Gus, the Christmas Mouse

By

Robert "Pa" Aldridge

Dedication

I dedicate "Gus, the Christmas Mouse" to the Aldridge clan: my children Parris, Mickie Beth, Rusty, and Tom; grandchildren, Shaun. Phillip, Dustin, Jake, Ian, Katie, and Kelley; great grandchildren Dusti, Bryce, Clint, Camden, and Ava Caroline; and to my great, great, grandchild to be born in September of 2014.

Acknowledgements

I acknowledge my Father, Tom, and Uncle Henry who taught me the art of storytelling, and to Mona Long who inspired me to finish the work I had started years before. And also to Yvonne Duncan who transcribed my scribbles into a manuscript, and my mentor, Bill Boudreau.

Life just didn't get much better than this!

Augustus T. Longtail enjoyed a good life. High in the hayloft of a cozy barn, he had a comfy nest, plenty of seeds scattered through the hay for him to eat, and lots of cousins to play chase along the rafters, Even the fierce, and always hungry, barn cat did not bother him. She was a floor dweller. High in the loft were hay tunnels where no cat could follow. Gus was wintering in style.

Gus paid no mind to snow drifts along the barn walls. December's cold winds, sweeping down from the Alpine peaks only lulled him to sleep as he curled up in his warm nest. For a mouse, life just didn't get much better than this.

One bright day, Gus awoke to strange noises. Something huge was in the loft. Floorboards creaked a warning as it came closer. He huddled quietly in his nest. Cat's eyes, his mother had told him, are attracted by motion. But they might miss seeing a mouse that was very still. This intruder seemed awfully big and noisy for a cat, but he'd take no chances, just lay motionless.

A sharp wooden prong just missed Gus!

It was not a cat making that noise. It was the farmer, Otto Katz, moving hay from the loft into the barn to feed his cows. He swung his heavy pitchfork, CRASH! Gus's nest was shaken. A great, sharp wooden prong slid through the hay, just missing Gus. His quivering body rumbled. Hay, nest, and Gus went sliding down a slanted ramp into the barn below. Tumbling, falling, he could not make his way back up to safety against the rush of moving hay. He landed, KERPLOP, amidst the hay in a big trough. He lay still, heart pounding wildly from shock and fear. A loud voice shattered the quiet. Gus perked up his ears. He had heard it before, but never so close. It was Farmer Katz, crooning to his milk cow. "Dar you are, Liebchin, nice sweet smelling hay for you to eat. We must have lots of fresh milk and rich cream for Mama's holiday baking. Eat, eat your fill, old cow, and make good sweet milk for her to use in her kitchen. Every creature should eat well, for Christmas is corning." Farmer Katz gave his cow a loving pat on her muzzle and scratched her ears. Then, humming a carol, he hunched his shoulders against the cold wind and went outside. Gus waited. Except for a strange crunching noise, all was quiet. Perhaps it would be safe for him to find out just where he was. He squirmed his way upward toward daylight.

Gus had never seen a cow up close before!

Munch, munch, the hay above Gus disappeared. He watched with awe as it vanished into the mouth of the biggest animal he had ever seen. A big brown eye gazed down on him as the huge jaws continued chewing, chewing. Gus had never seen a cow up close before. His blood ran cold. He had no idea that she was as surprised as he was.

With a terrified squeak, Gus leaped atop the trough. He landed running. The ramp down which he had slipped was closed denying him access to safety above.

Gus dodged his way through the hay; putting as much distance as possible between himself and that huge, scary beast.

The barn cat was uncurling from her bed, yawning, stretching, and preparing to hunt him. Gus's squeak had been a big mistake. She had heard it. She was coming after him; her green eyes glowing like lamps. Gus must hide! There was no safe place on the barn floor. She could catch him there.

He was too fearful of becoming cow's dinner to seek concealment in the feed trough. He couldn't stay where he was. That cat was already sniffing, testing the air for some trace of mouse. She would find him soon if he didn't move.

Desperately, Gus looked around. He saw a glimmer of light. One shutter had a broken corner leaving a mouse-sized exit to safety outside.

The cat sprang after him!

As Gus jumped for the hole, the cat sprang after him. Without an instant to spare, he wriggled through and dropped onto a snowdrift beneath. Looking up, he could see the cat's paw, cruel claws extended, reaching out, groping, searching, hunting him. That was close!

As far as Gus could see there was snow, unbroken except for the trunks of tree towering above. A cold wind ruffled his pelt and sent icy particles into his eyes and ears. Where could he go? Where could he be warm? Moaning Alpine winds gave him no answer.

It was a hard winter for all forest creatures!

Gus' feet were freezing!

Gus scurried along the snowdrift. The cat had declined to leave the warm barn to hunt Gus outside. Even so, he knew instinctively, there was danger here. Owls hunted mice, so did weasels. The mind numbing cold was a danger too. He had to keep moving, had to seek shelter and food. The snow was wind crusted. Gus's feet left no tracks and found no traction. He could make good speed as long as he went straight ahead, but when he tried to turn and dart among logs in a woodpile, he tumbled.

Trying, he found that he could steer himself with his tail. Slinging his tail left, he turned right. When he slung it to the right, he turned left. But, no matter which way he turned, he could find no place to hide, rest, or get warm. His feet were freezing.

It was a hard winter for all forest creatures. Even prudent gray squirrels lost their hidden hoards of food under the snow. Hidden away in a hole in a rock fence, a hungry weasel planned his hunt. Everything looked like dinner to him — a snow bird roosting, a sleepy squirrel, or a juicy mouse. The weasel's nose twitched. He smelled a mouse.

"How unusual," the weasel thought. Most mice would be hidden away in their snug nests. His nose was not often fooled. He knew a mouse when he smelled one. He poked his pointed snout out of his lair.

The rising moon reflected off the snow making it almost as bright as day. The weasel sniffed the wind. He could see no trail, but his nose told him where Gus had run across the icy surface. His sinuous body slithered out into the cold. He would have a mouse for his evening meal.

As the weasel left his den, another hunter was watching Gus. High on a snowy tree limb sat an owl, his large yellow eyes scanning for any trace of motion on the moonlit snow. He had seen Gus darting from shadow to shadow, searching for a safe place to rest.

Gus saw a clearing ahead. It it was a building. Was it another cozy barn? He would investigate.

Owl tensed, he did not want to fly off into the wind. He would turn on his perch, allow his prey to pass under him, and then glide downwind for the kill.

Gus's scent grew stronger in weasel's nostrils. He could see movement on the snow ahead. He ran faster along Gus's trail.

The weasel ran faster along Gus' trail!

Gus was growing very tired. He was so cold. "What is the use?" he thought. "I can't outrun this cold wind." He looked over his shoulder. To Gus' horror, the weasel was running. It was only a few yards behind him. Sheer terror flushed all thoughts of giving up. He ran for his life. Through the snow crust he could feel weasel's feet pounding as it readied to spring.

Quick thinking, Gus gave his tail a hard twist to the right, throwing him into a skidding left turn. Just at that moment, he passed beneath the limb on which owl waited.

Weasel sprang. Owl Swooped. There was a terrified squeal and a squawk as fur and feathers flew. Both hunters had missed Gus when he turned. Owl had buried his sharp talons into weasel's back. Weasel was fighting with tooth and claw to keep from being carried away. As they fought, Gus scrambled toward the building he had seen.

Gus had found a country church!

It didn't smell like a barn. He searched for a way to get in. There were no loose boards, no holes that he could find. He climbed a wall. Here, at least, he was sheltered from the chilling wind. The roof was so steep that all snow had slipped from the shingles. Wind noise told him there was another structure rising from the roof. He climbed again.

Instead of a solid wall, here was a wooden lattice. He squeezed through a hole. Gus had found the bell tower of a country church. Dangling from the bell, a rope led into the silent room below.

He began to explore!

It was cold and dark, but the wind could not reach him here. He began to explore. There were rows of plain wooden benches, In front was a table, a pulpit, and an organ. Hungry, Gus sniffed for something to eat. The floor was clean and bare. He found no food among the benches. The table was empty, except for a big closed book lying in the center. Gus went to the organ.

He sniffed along the keys, and then stopped. He peeked at pipes. Finally he crawled over foot pedals into the instrument's heart where a great leather bellows stored air which was forced through the pipes to make music.

There he found something he could eat. Tallow dripping from a candle had left a glob on the tough leather. Gus began to gnaw hungrily. His sharp teeth tore the wax soaked leather. Soon there was a large hole in the bellows.

Warm at last and with a full stomach, Gus fell asleep. Sometime later, he was awakened by voices.

Pastor Grubber said, "The wind has stopped. We will have a beautiful night for our Christmas Eve services, all calm and bright."

Gus lay very still. Someone was coming nearer to Gus' hiding place. "What hymns would you like for me to play? Oh! I can hardly wait to fill the night with joyful music."

He sat on the organ bench; put his feet on the pedals as he adjusted stops with his hands. He began to pedal, SWOOSH air escaped through the hole Gus had eaten in the bellows. Swoosh, swoosh was all the sound the organ would make.

"What is this? What is wrong with my organ?" He asked in a whisper, dropping to his hands and knees, peering into the instrument.

"Pastor, there's a hole in the bellows!"

"Pastor, Pastor, there is a hole in the bellows. It cannot be played. Oh! We shall have no music for Christmas Eve. What a shame, what a shame it is, Pastor, that this most holy night must remain silent."

He rocked in quiet anguish, back and forth on the organ bench as another man entered.

"What is this, Heinrich, is there something wrong with the organ?" he asked in a soft voice.

Together they examined the damaged bellows. Gus's dinner had left it unable to contain air.

"I don't think it can be repaired in time for tonight. How can we sing to honor the holy child with no organ?"

"Well," mused Pastor Franz Gruber, "the organ is useless, it is true. I do, however, still have an old guitar from my student days. Perhaps I can play something on it that we all could sing."

Heinrich sighed mightily, bundled himself in coat and muffler, pulled his cap over his ears, and eased out the door.

Rising softly, pastor Gruber went to his closet. There, far in the back was his guitar. Lovingly he picked up the worn instrument and strummed a chord. "It is a bit out of tune, but I can remedy that," he thought. Hands that had not played music for years still remembered the chords. When he was satisfied with the sound he wandered back into the sanctuary and sat on the organ bench.

"What was it that Heinrich said, 'What a shame that this most holy night should be silent?' Maybe not — it might be that after the angelic chorus, after the shepherds had worshipped and departed, there came a time of blessed silence, so mother and child could sleep. Even the animals would be quiet.

Peace and goodwill would reign over the land and people.

It was on that Christmas Eve, with none to listen but a sleepy mouse, that Franz Gruber strummed *his* guitar alone in the gloom of an empty church, composing our beloved Christmas Carol, *"SILENT NIGHT."*

About the Author

Robert "Pa" Aldridge is a card carrying picture toting grandfather. A native Oklahoman, he developed the art of storytelling to entertain his children, and later, his grandchildren. After 30 years in the retail business, he retired and began to put on paper the countless tales he had spun to keep from hearing the dread phrase, "Are we there yet?"

About the Graphic Artist

Strangely enough I have never met Miss Jade Huang who did the original artwork for this book. Jade and her mother were in the program at Brevard County Rescue Mission. I had asked Miss Victoria Glavas, a volunteer at the Mission, if she was interested in doing the artwork for Gus. She was busy getting ready to attend University of Florida; but mentioned that she had seen Jade's work and been impressed.

So I sent Jade a copy of the manuscript with the instructions to portray Gus as she saw him in her mind's eye. The result is the illustrations that enliven the story. Jade is sixteen years old.

I envision a successful career for her in the field of graphic arts.

CPSIA information can be obtained at www.ICGtesting.com
Printed in the USA
BVIW12n0215171116
468150BV00016B/69